Magic Happens!
(inside of you)

Laurie Fisher Huck

ELEMENT
CHILDREN'S BOOKS

SHAFTESBURY, DORSET · BOSTON, MASSACHUSETTS · MELBOURNE, VICTORIA

First published in the UK in 1998 by
Element Children's Books, Shaftesbury, Dorset SP7 8BP

Published in Australia in 1998 by Element Books Ltd for
Penguin Books Australia Ltd, 487 Maroondah Highway,
Ringwood, Victoria 3134

First published in 1996 by Weatherhill, Inc, of New York
and Tokyo, 568 Broadway, Suite 705, New York, NY10012

British Library Cataloguing in Publication data available

ISBN 1 901881 09 1

Cover design by Ness Wood
Printed in Hong Kong through Worldprint

To my best friend.

This book is about magic.

Not fairy tale...
Trust me, baby.

...rabbit-in-a-hat...

...abracadabra...

I told those *@# creeps not to use any starch!
MEGA
...comic book magic.

This
book
is
about

Real
magic.

Ordinary magic.
Ordinary!!??
MEGA

Magic that lives inside...
Inside?

of

You

Have you ever had this feeling?

Say you're walking down the stairs...

...in your star-studded socks,

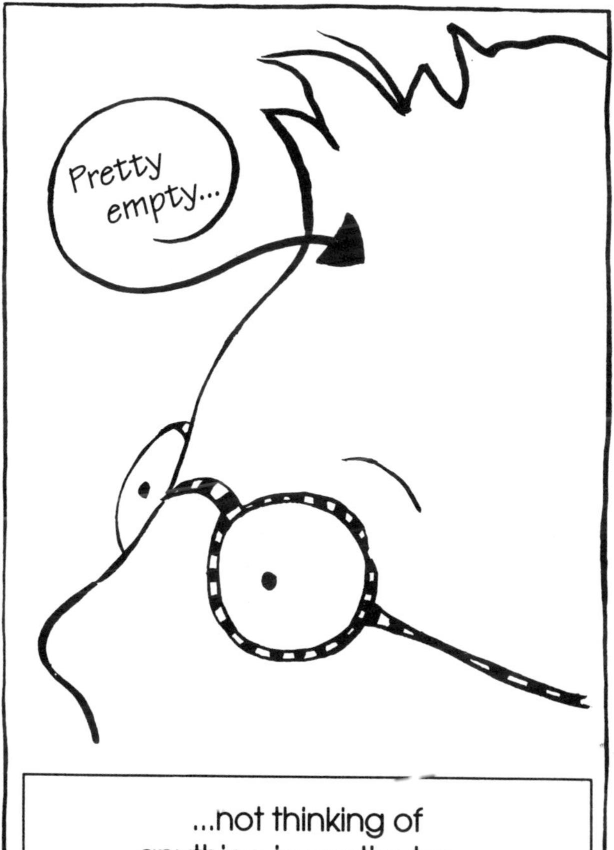
Pretty empty...
...not thinking of anything in particular....

PFTT!
...when suddenly...

...your mind just stops...

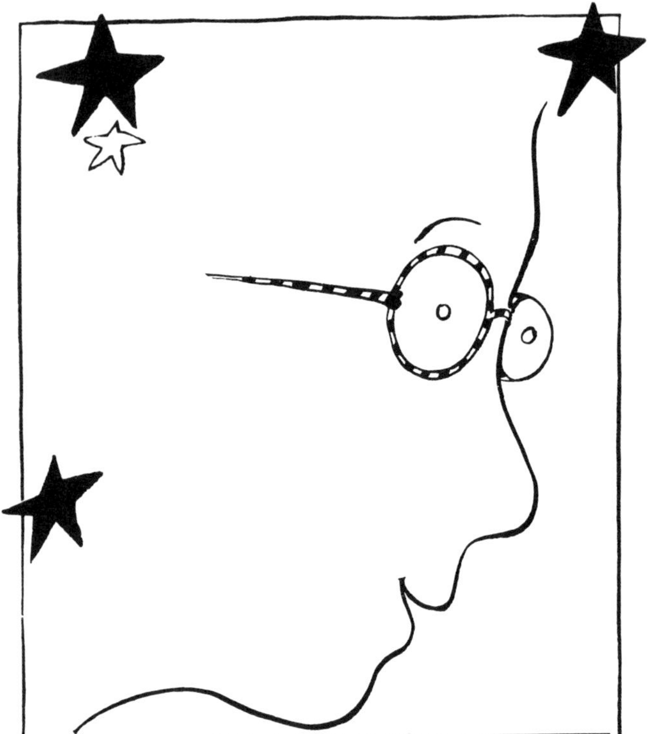

...and feels as big,
and as empty
as space.

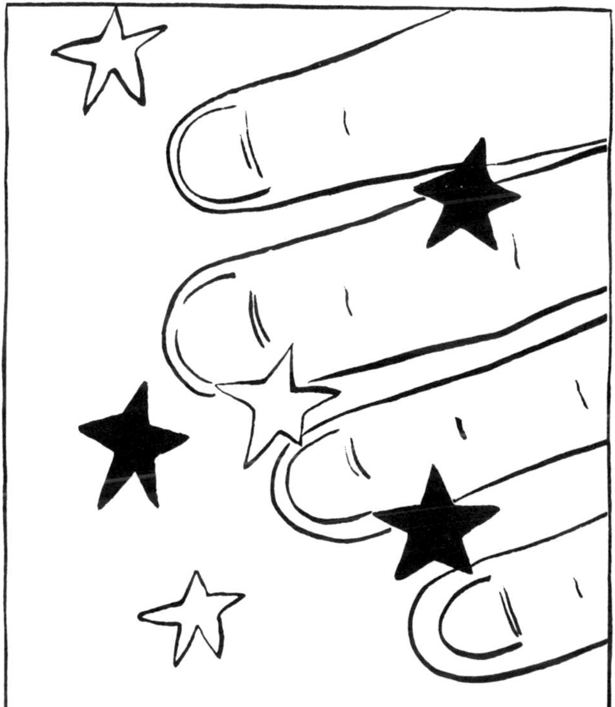

Things feel
so-o-o-o-o-o clear
your whole body tingles...

...and a little bit about
this world makes sense.
YES!

WOW! What is that feeling?

That's Magic

A treasure hunt.

I'm ready.
How do I get there?
MAGIC MAP
GUARANTEED

Relax,

you're
already there.

But...how can I make magic happen?

Simple,

by
just
being
who
you
are.

Not who you think you are.

Not who you think you should be.
I'll save the world!
Oh my... WAKE UP!

Quite simply,
who you are.

Because who you really are
...is magic.
Okay. Tell me. Who am I really?

Good question.

The basics.

You
are
a
human
being.

You have a body...

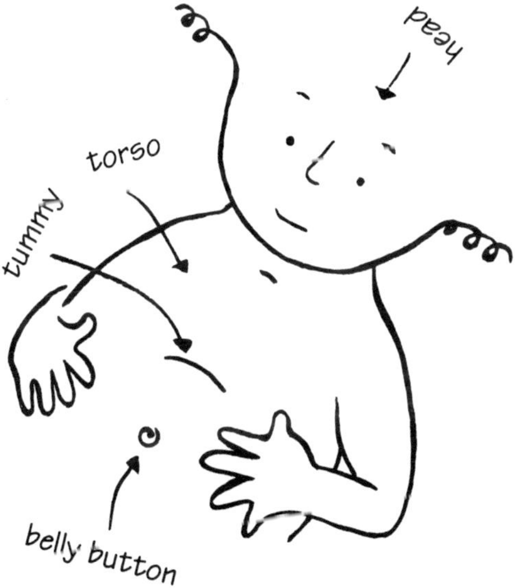

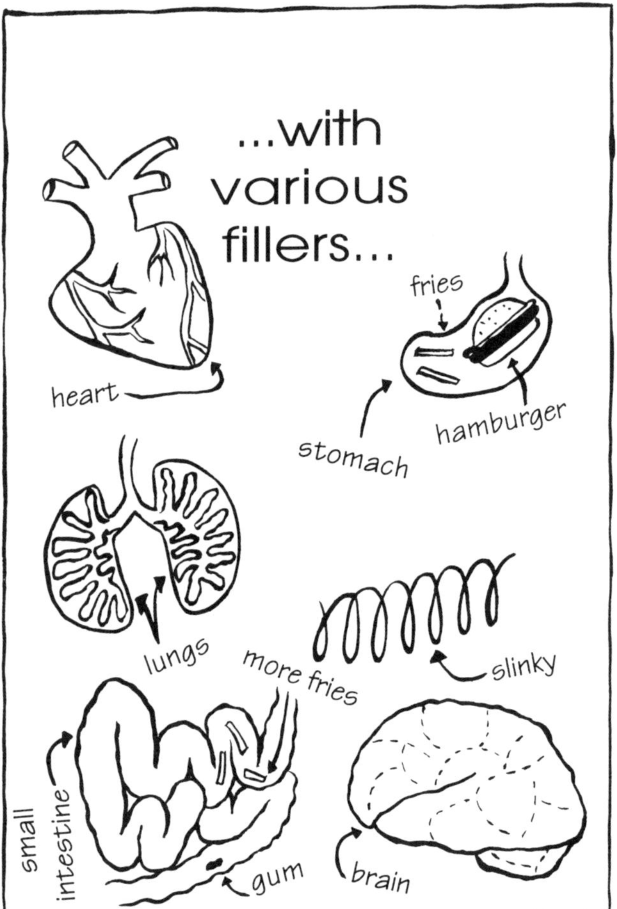
...with various fillers...
heart
fries
stomach
hamburger
lungs
more fries
slinky
small intestine
gum
brain

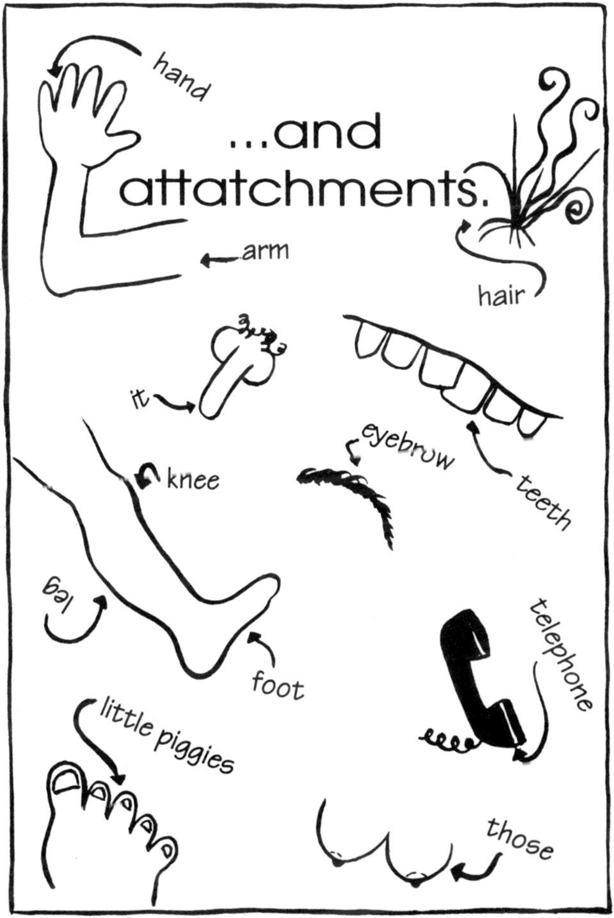
...and
attatchments.
hand
arm
hair
it
teeth
eyebrow
knee
leg
foot
telephone
little piggies
those

You
have
a
mind

This thought is happening

that is
light,
clear,
and vast…

in a vast, empty space...

...where thoughts come and go...

...and you
have
senses...that sense.
Yum!
peppermint
chocolate chip
slurp

Plus...

You have a heart full of wisdom and basic goodness.

It shines like the sun

in a brilliant, clear sky.

All these things help
you go out and
touch your world...
Hello world

...and let the world come in and touch you.

So you see,

just
being
you
is
Magic.

No way!
Yikes!

Way.

A magic check.

Have you ever had a moment when your heart has been really, truly, genuinely touched?

It feels
kind of
soft and squishy,
sad and happy,
full and empty,
all at once.

Maybe
you want to cry
or hug someone.

Maybe
you have a
brilliant idea.

Maybe
you feel happy
just being alive.

Maybe
you feel
enlightened.

Everyone experiences moments like these.

Everyone has a heart that can be touched.

When

your
basic
human
goodness

and
the
world
meet,

that's magic.

On
the
spot.

Hey wait!
How come sometimes
I feel so.....you know...
BAD?

Ah yes...
clouds.

They come...they go...
and occasionally...
...they cover the sun.

In this case,
the
clouds
are the
yakkety-yak
of
your
very
own
mind.

Howdy doodey there.
I'm just an old yakkety yak from the Himalayas.
Yep I sure do like to yak, you know, living up here in the old Himis it's fun to keep the old mind busy, that's what I always say. I mean who cares that there's a whole world happening when I can just be listening to myself yak yak yak. Yessiree bob, nothing like it. I don't have to feel anything or notice anything. I can just yak my head off to myself and I never even have to know what anyone else is thinking and that way I don't ever have to do anything. I mean yeah sure maybe I don't have any friends but you know it's scarey to be who you are, I mean maybe you have to tell the truth or create something beautiful... but you know that's a lot of work and I am, after all, just a yakkety yak so I think I'll just stay here in my heap of stinky hair and keep yakking away and hope that someday I'll get to go to Florida. You know it's cold here in these Himis. That's what I call 'em. The Himis.
Yessirreebob...

Have you ever been in a beautiful place full of sunlight, trees, magic...

...then sam said he heard of a guy who fired off a ROCKET
powered with SUGAR CANE...now that's COOL...i mean...TALK
about a SUGAR HIGH...HA!...boy, HA HA am i FUNNY...TOO
BAD Tiffany DOESN'T THINK SO...what a BUMMER she
won't go with me...i mean, she thinks i'm shallow and she comes
up with things like ..."Am i pretty?"........."BUT...am i
PRETTY, pretty?"......i mean, what's THAT supposed to
mean?...GIVE ME A BREAK... oh well, i DON'T CARE...i'm going
into SPACE anyway...with 50 billion other galaxies i'm sure
there's a population with my kind of humor...besides, it's mega
boring sun...one moom...one PUNY ALLOWANCE...
HA! ...i think i'll build my own rocket...
YEAH!...and i'll get Tiffany ...she's really good at
science...and then MAYBE i th the Hubble on
internet by then...WHY NOT er telescopes on-line
and i can use the one at enever i want...Oh
yuck...i can't stand that ays there though...he
thinks he's so cool and calls in front of
everyone...face it, other day
that
...and your mind is somewhere
completely different...

...when quietly,
you and the world meet...

...and you wake up...

...to where you are right now?

Wow.

Even
if
there
are

clouds
in
the
sky...

...that
sun of
basic
goodness
is always
shining.

When you

slow down,

relax
your mind,

and
just be,

it's there...

...in the

most quiet,

most clear,

most gentle,

most awake,

most you,

spot inside you.

Magic

happens...

...when you
touch
this
spot.

A note from the author

The best way I know to relax the mind and experience magic is to meditate. There's a lot of "tricky magic" in the world that we just make up. I know. I've done it. Real magic is much more simple than that. Once you start seeing it, your whole life can become richer... not just the highs...everything.

Laurie Fisher Huck.

Picture of the author

(...on land after many years at sea.)